Land Sparing

Gabriella Klein

Land Sparing

Dómine, de rore
de pinguédin
, & defidéria
tuæ mileratió
m ergo nostr
ncti ficáre d
ut benedícere
raham, & If
arietes do m

Winner of the 2013 Nightboat Poetry Prize

NIGHTBOAT BOOKS
NEW YORK

© 2015 by Gabriella Klein
All rights reserved
Printed in the United States

ISBN 978-1-937658-32-8

Cover & interior art:
William Dole. *Second Architectural Fragment*, 1959.
Collage on canvas. Courtesy of John and Hilary Klein.

Design and typesetting by Margaret Tedesco
Text set in Apollo and Christiana

Cataloging-in-publication data is available
from the Library of Congress

Distributed by University Press of New England
One Court Street
Lebanon, NH 03766
www.upne.com

Nightboat Books
New York
www.nightboat.org

For my family tree

Contents

The future was
successive and successful answers to those
questions it made sense to ask. How far from the
earth itself could we project? And what was light?

James McMichael
Four Good Things

Plainsong

Tree lined and transatlantic,
I was impatient, Earth,
for cataclysmic feats.
To reckon with the reckless
behavior. My feet on the train seat.
The mind obsesses on teleology,
how it will end and for what sake.
Tremor and flood. Ascension.
One last smoke.
Beneath the greenleaf awning,
the night's cracked plaster,
the hereafter.
To live rejoicing and true-footed.
A common prayer. Place your
all you ever wanted into me.

Coffin Bone

The loom inside a horse, the engine
that drives thrashing
on great slabs of neck. Anger at god

is not god. The Appaloosa
is refusing to cross thresholds,
neither in nor out as dementia

is a dethroned king.
Comes Trouble gives up in the field. Why,
I confess to his peaceful

head flat to grass. If the mud elongates
the tendon, the coffin bone
will stride through the hoof. A constellation

traverses the horseshoe meadow. The insects
are a cacophony of amity.
We'll rope you to a tractor and pull.

The Firmament

The universe was initially all hydrogen,
pure longing. Cosmology's original sin.

Charge parity, symmetry, once violated,
is impossible to regain.
Mostly you break your own heart.

Helium, lithium, beryllium, in order.
The outer electrons we lose and gain.

A quark has six flavors.
You will wonder to whom I speak.
Up, down, strange, charm, bottom, top.
Infatuation with the night tears you up.

All matter is supposed to equal anti-matter
but it doesn't. Those laws are lawless.
I mistook you for midnight,
the listing trees. But who is to say.

Boron, carbon, nitrogen.
The night was spaceship silver
with white owls in the oaks.
We were lying in the leaves, in the stars.

Stellarium

Seen from a distance
dissimilars become similar.

The light is light and space.

We crawl out and
back into the sea.

The light is neon, amniotic,
pouring through.

We deliquesce and what is left?

The silver gelatin prints, the palms

with long fronds of hair thrown back
as the slender things of stardom.

Consensus

What if we can't wake to birdsong and what if

of the weather

we are afraid?

Afraid you will leave me.

Our daughter thinks

until I explain

she only came from me.

The sky rains and rain

all the more becomes the sea.

Each time the body

reproduces itself,

then outgrows itself.

My, my. We have been in the wind a long time.

Land Use

I have never seen half the things I have read.

Nor spoken of.

A mosquito's diseased proboscis.

Feathers in a typhoid lake.

When just last night the world was a party.

Nothing is as it should be at the time.

You had no idea

you had this idea.

The winged beetles will survive

another million years. Earth, take me with you.

Bracket

Your bliss, a footnote.
What is more enduring?

Parenthetically, I have seen
in your eyes.

That you believe
the reflexive. That I believe you.

Define degradation.
A tree lying down

becomes a sentence.

Orthography won't save us.
Delete, delete.

Free, Works

You are just another relative,
grinding coffee and staining cups.

In the garage
a drawer full of chisels.

A drawerful. What did I marry?

Hallways bruised with furniture.
Who put that there?

We planted a garden
we will all water. Who will I raise?

Inter Alia

Define a forest. The men who meant to.

The houses I have lived in and left.

With unnatural affection for the warped glass.

The waves sound like the freeway

and the cars mimic the sea.

We are living on a pain and pleasure planet.

I have countries to see.

I insisted, Earth,

upon your kinship.

Have I written sufficiently? We are all talk.

A Camino.
B Caminiera.
C Porta.
D Sopra porta
E Scudo y il Braciale

Elsewhere Desire

As soon as you read of the boom you read

they have moved on. The gamblers, the outlaws,

the Argonauts in a cold stream.

The miners are ghosts. The mines have been deserted.

Those lawless quick towns, the fabricated.

Once there were prospects, now there is sky, and elsewhere

desire has moved on.

Desert your expectation. A ghost town is nothing less.

The wallpaper frayed, the stamped tin

corroded. Boredom and its reflection in glass.

I fill it up with muttering but still I am alone.

Except for heartbreak. Sometimes a hunger

means chewing your own cheek.

Monotony, monotony. What I call gold.

Time Dilation

We have seen so little, we have
invented so much.
Having worked by starlight
to map the abstract, the usual
dimensions.
Length, breadth, width
and duration.
A lighted disc in a darkened sky.
Time is not independent of motion.
It dilates and does not stand still.
You catch the flying object
both where and when.
In the blueness of space
we will transubstantiate.
Pools to gasses.
Mercury's day
is longer than his year.
See the clock hands hurry to catch up.

Bruximania

You think past midnight your heartbeat is an earthquake.
The blood rivers pulse and, frantic, you set fires
to contain the fires. To sleep without tending to sleep.

List maker, let failure be its own garden.
Bury the accidents. Eden
is a worry plot with nude trees vining

everything that can and will
go wrong. The intersection
of yes and no at which you meant to stop.

Do you love me, I ask me, or do I make you
lonely? Unlock your jaw. It is worth repeating.
A forehead held in fever, now we are kin.

Nobody Is Cabrillo Anymore

Leagues ago I was alone on the island.
Bird skin dress. A nest watcher.
I was alone for fathoms,
a ringing in my ears.
To sing is to travel. The open bay
offers no safety, sail on.

Before the gold rush was before
the port belonged
to exploration,
its own treasure beyond finding
a salt marsh, the Bay of Smoke.
We're not taking
formal possession.

The chaparral is burning,
I ache a gangrenous leg.
We need hides more than money,
that useless pocketing,
something to hole up
this ringing in my ears.
You know wildness
can infect horses already broken.

When we have learned the island sufficient we will go.

Street Light

I would bend for you.
The underground rivers
veining a city.
Beneath which streets.
Muddied
with eventual rain.
Weeds cupping
waist high.
I would undress for you.
For all that I was
at the time
too young to learn.
What sin is.
The river daylights.
You wish you had not wanted
flooding in spring.

The Honeycomb Conjecture

If a bee is busy, too busy
to feel woe. Or the absence
of pollen, which is to say, lonely.
I would lie with you
in the open road.
As a bee's light
we are a premise untested.
Some forces act upon the nucleus
while others extend.
Massless particles, messengers.
Inside us
lives a colony of space.
Grief can be
both fungus and virus.
The holes regret fills.
Unborn, unwritten,
unmet, unsaid.
Nectar adhering
to static and fuzz.
Hive collapse is nearly.
We are losing our ability
to navigate home.

Carry Your Error

It is customary to measure
below the trunk's swelling.

Diameter at breast height.
What a tree holds.

Timber volume. Opened
like a sternum, broke a bone.

I might be all wrong.
Consider a misstep

early on in the equation.
I stole a belt I never wore.

Nothing can circle me.
Long lacy leafy limbs.

Girthing tape and calipers.
I darken my eyes.

Like I already came for you
asking for more. For what more?

Comes Trouble

Bright now is fading

the sun worn strip, the soda pop sky.

You meet on a racetrack and can't recollect

the beginning to what has no end.

It elongates, it elastics.

Along the perimeter is all

we have. Shed wings, you'll grow wings.

Considers That

Whereas parties have agreed upon
previously enacted platforms, including
broad participation. Including robust behavior.
Request that the safeguards referred to are being addressed.
Be consistent that, should the wind derive
from the west, all subsequent actions be adjusted.
Recognize that the sun will at times be obscured
by the imminence of a storm. Acknowledge that
not everything you love belongs to you.
Address the risk of reversal. Report on progress made.
Agree to show restraint or to bracket the impossibility.
By taking into account guidance,
by laying down the body alongside the river
just before it rains.
By ensuring that in doing so, it will never rain.
The grass will measure your longing. The cottonwood
cotton will lather the sky. The river will flow north
in the context of the provision.
Further decide that lightning need not always summon rain.
Invite parties to consider the alternative.
Admit the alternative does not yet exist.
Develop modalities in accordance with the decision
to sallow down in the grass. To slow, halt
and reverse loss. Recalling
the feel of trunk bark. Recalling the nights unspent.

eis , Dómine , de rore
m , & de pinguédin
tiam , & desidéria
ctum tuæ miseratió
m ergo nostr
ncti ✠ ficáre d
:ut benedícere
:raham , & Is
arietes domu

You Are a Bird of Paradise

With our excess lust we travel,
money we drink,

oil we drive.

I lean my attention to the road
like a needle darning traffic.

What if I love you too much?

We affix the bad news with advertisement.

Filling a human inch of sky.

Flags, balloons tethering
cars for sale. Trucks for sale.

Technology is ruining my handwriting
but not my sense of smell. Night-blooming,

we arrive to the slowing in the southbound lane.

Minifauna

I'm nostalgic for sweet peas in May, but here I am
buying sweet peas
in rag bouquets. How long

has it been June?

If ever
you look up and I am starting to cry,

if instead of color
all I want is light.
The world's fodder whited out.

Your heart cleaves its chambers.
It will always turn summer in my mind.

A bog, a saturation.
The ferns blur, inconstant. Lichen

electric on the bark.
Humidity beseeches. Even if, even then.

Where the road
settles to grass, I'll be waiting in the six pm sun.

Mean Temperature

Should the wind sheen down at sundown
the aloes will be unmoved.
I am taken with your talons,
your volatile oils
to purge and sooth.
As wind precedes fire
and fire precedes new.
Unruly dragon tongues, bright
blooms in winter. Rosettes of flesh.
To prepare for loss we must
practice mourning. I miss you.
I miss you. The brief season.
Your hand on my pulse.
We grow how we grow
with a girth of reminiscence.
When we were younger.
When we sat by the pool.
Dear aloes. I was waiting for this.
Red pendants born at the apex.
For all our work that goes unseen.
We adapt to specificity. Earth,
your love spells me. I will rake the path clean.

Covers its Nudity, Lives Under a Roof

Tuck here,

a pleat, this undressing.

Who wants a soldier on leave

one night, no blaming.

Unhook your corset. Charge rent.

It's not like other wars she says

to the sink, the yellow bathrobe, no one

has taken an enemy wife.

In god's Once we were roomless.

No molding or mourning dress or trim.

What did we dream in? Voile

on the veranda, ruched silk.

I've seen you leave in uniform. Return

in uniform. Brother, son, grandson. We dreamt of

airfields and decoration. Let out your blueprint, your fraying hem.

River Begin Again

I floated in tires, in jellies,

in August.

Cupping the current in handfuls

to ease the burn.

I was also a child.

Before the skies

humidly graying,

before we reached the break and bulk.

And will it never,

for your daughter,

thunder?

You ask that future

version of yourself.

The one you left a car for

downstream.

The Tell

The past is a lit city
with a flag that says, encore.

I'll weep at anything,
the blow down in the woods.

War is a long lie. New lies
make the old lies true.
People aren't staying in their skin.

A man is arrested for hunting deer
out of season. For out of season

hunting geese and grouse.
The pumpkins collapse.
I drift down the driveway

behind the windshield,
turn off the engine, don't open the door.

Chinook Stand Still

Bare lilac alleys,
days in whiteness
like a gestation, a six-month mood.
Alone on a snowdrift, melting,
the ground flooded with sudden.
All winter bitten with cold.
Mothers, you should wake for this prairie.
Ice break on the river
severs free a drift and floe.
Wind erasing, dear Chinook,
an entire season's snow.
I remove my hat, my scarf,
my gloves. Skin is breathing as if
newborn. I wanted to be
Blackfoot and beaded.
The edges are disappearing.
It agitates you to be so strong.

By My Stars

There were condom machines in the washroom
when you drove me
upstate. The roadside
loosestrife in our headlights. And the fireweed,
the August humid heat transfer. Your hand
on the gearshift. I gave myself
to your nightdriving and slept.

In my long wish, Earth, it is
sea after sea, with shocking shifting plates.
I'd sail all over you.
If you ask me to.
For the severalth time tonight
the rain lets up. With heat plucking steam from the leaves.

Pond

The lazy center
is a green neither
sharp nor fading, reminding

not of before nor after.
Picture the waterweeds have always been this high.

This July fable, forever
verdant and felt. For once

a war has not been sighted,
is not negotiating the daily toll.

Come home is not a letter home.

The dock is weathered but from what weather?
The velvet moss
but when did it grow?

Perfection will disallow memory. Take your pick,
the mind is full of ponds.

I wore the dock smooth just by imagining

summer, close your eyes.

Comes True

A pulse of red occurring
in the Northern Light sky

and the mind

that will never be of winter
thinks first of wildfire

a mindless
cold snap

possible rain, possible

freezing rain
it occurs to me

in any measured form
there will be one stray thought

like the horse that wanders off.

Black Sea

The day was fine and soon it will be
that you never left our bed.

Busy looking, looking. Busy watching
down a tunnel
for a train.

The windows were open all day.

A train of rivers,
mouths gaping into oceans.

A river of trains

in the blue dusk light.
Waiting for an arrival

or the departure of day.
Go on believing

a train will come
to carry the wreckage away.

A Camino.
B Caminiera.
C Porta.
D Sopra porta
E Scudo y il Braciale

Myopia

Extinction will validate
the technophile.
Our accurate modeling.
Allometry and isometry.
That of which
we can infer.
Having loved you
from a distance and in good light.
A string of bare bulbs.
Do not mistake catastrophe
for impatience
for our demise. Tireless spinning.
The weather skin.
The nights grow dendrometric.
Wood density, age,
thickness of bark.
Factor in human tendency
for error.
You learn to read by being
read to. It's not yet dawn.

To Every Mothlike Promise

Summer is not ever the way summer is
and June's a novocain
to every mothlike promise. It won't
hurt much, this chrysalis, this evolution.
We are aging like a planet. Even you
drove the ice cream truck.

We wash our scraped knees with chlorine and
don't run on the splashed cement.
Pool city, pool time. We are
caught in the rainstorm we saw coming
across the prairie sky. Cosmos gray and shining,
the hail tooth-size around us. Where summer sits
inside a downpour and heat and lightning take us in,
make us scramble from the pool like footage in reverse.

To get better at pain is not the same
as numbness, or a temporary loss
of sun. How watery fathers can be
on the edge, adjusting goggles, at any age.

The Jet Stream

You wake in the morning
and it is night.
Time has flown.
Ghosts cling to the plane
like a glossary of terms.
The Coriolis force
is proportional to the rotation rate.
The centrifugal force is proportional
to its square.
We are, in human form,
better suited for migration,
to follow the herds and the rains.
A shift in the hemisphere
and water appears to veer,
blood too is coursing, counter
clockwise. Spinning,
as it were in childhood,
to disrupt the inertia.
You wake in the night
and it is morning. Time has flown.

Diagonal of a Rectangle

There are things I can't figure out
if this
comma
then

how do the deer overwinter over winter
there is no
food
repeat
there is no food

the length of day is measured
against the width of night

which is greater than yesterday
and less than tomorrow

figure a line drawn
from the pinnacle of a mountain to its base

and the distance between
parenthesis
among
parenthesis
trees

from the summit
the world is

snow dash ice dash clouds dash fog

if all this gray
equals love beauty etcetera

if comma then
why are you crying again?

The Glow in the Dark

The wind in the lone palm

like water upon water. Rain

on a nightblack lake.

I'll never tire of you.

The eaves rain

and the undersides of leaves.

Why do words strip you down?

I can see from here

to the islands.

The channel opens, the swimmable haze.

Timelessness without revelation.

Nothing to confess.

The Wash I Fold

She had a broom collection.
Individually

there is not much left by the end.

Bones, blood
pressure. Knowledge of rare

snow on the chaparral.

The rest, rest
your wordless
eyes.

Everything we do we undo.

The dishes I wash, the wash I fold.

She goes back to bed before breakfast
after filling the tray with water

to make ice.

The Weather Our Father

I'm on the sand,
he's on the boardwalk.

The sky is gauzy,
impeccably still.

Some droughts we own
more than others.

Pity, small talk.

But we've been to the sea
like yesterday

and tomorrow. Take my sadness,
we all cried, and my sorrow.

The talk of no rain.
The talk of sun.

Summit

The mountain begins
paces from your waking.

Delicate mosses
in glacial retreat.

Lapland rosebay,
resilience

I always flock to.
The lichens

wed to rock.
I won't make you talk about it

until we get it right.
The trees give way

to a tundra meadow
shattered all morning by wind.

Space Opera

Prove we live in a galaxy

in which we are a fertile thought.

Me in my bed and you in yours.

Hands that shuttle me.

Come back, Earth,

my undying.

I swept the stairwell for you.

Something other than words appears

beautiful for the first time.

To a Stranger World

The best the dusk
can offer. A stand of black locust
silhouetting rain.

The band is unpacking. The bandstand glows. Everyone
you used to know.

The moon would be corn high. We should be
picking fruit
in a sleep-tiered meadow,

but for the storm. Was
louder than tympani, louder than horns.

Trumpets, tubas, marching across nightfields.

Parts Per Million

A hurricane on Jupiter
the size of Earth.
Words won't do.

The unfinished crossword, the science behind
the wind behind the storm.

Save us from measure. Never the right weather.

The oriole traffic used to stop
in the backfield.

Do you miss what you do not hear?

A flock, a sedge, an unkindness.
Lesser migration, it must be imagined.

Like the future. Don't stop. We want
winter again, and summer.

We want as many, as all.

Minus Tide

Were I
to work precisely.
Were I to
score more.
Why, regarding,
I want to
and should not,
incanting frenzy,
touch your rough hair.
There ever
to go unspent
our good fortune.
A fair coined exchange.

Coast Starlight

I saw a whale spout
but no whale.
You were never
mine to define.
The electroweak theory,
a mental migration,
was hastened along.
We have nothing
to hide from
each other.
I can neither prove
nor disprove the whale.
We cobble together
like gulls to grunion.
As if god were a particle.
And proof is nigh.
The tides peel
like milk and flatten.
I like the feel, Earth,
of being spun.

Earthquake Weather

The insects swarming backwards
and the hearts I wish I'd broken.

Content is the grass.

Set your love down
when you die. A crow in metronome.

Virgin Forest

Wind in a low moan
like ghosts in the thousands.
Inelegant vapor.
Like I opened a sieve.
Given the circumstance.
Like a primer.
I erase all my mistakes.
He was improbable.
I waited on him
all summer
long.
It began, one day
he sat under the patio
umbrella having
drinks. Drinks. Having drinks.

The House of Ups and Downs

The evidence of past years
rain in the wallseep like an acid comedown
when colors

don't hold fast.
You are clutching the banister you are shaking.

Each eye a festering mind.

We live in inherited
matter. Starch,
cellulose, addiction.

Something must be eaten
for something else to grow.

Like killing pain with pain. Good morning cousin.

The Valley of Elephants

You are sitting on a chair in a room in a mission
on a mountain
near the ocean.

Because it happened
does not mean it will happen again.

A forest is like a cliff driven herd.

Earth, I love your ten million wounded.

I confess my sinning
on the church steps.

The mere idea of ground.

Time Lapse Museum

Losing quarters to a poker machine
quicker than rain and the day
condenses to a flash.
You count beats until thunder and then
it's all over.
The spoons are laid, licked clean,
removed to the sink faster than sizzle.
You can't have heyday without decline
racing through the old hotel.
Chairs fill and empty drought-like.
There is no more gold.
We buried our dust and in haste
have forgotten where.
A ghost town is nothing more.
Call it admiration, this desolation. Some towns
will never be towns again. About the gold rush,
all the lies were true. No one hesitates. It's all on film.

A Camino.
B Caminiera.
C Porta.
D Sopra porta.
E Scudo g il Brac

A Grief Magnetic

The moon's ever black sky and ever quiet.
Not even sadness

makes a sound. It is time
to stop crying.

We are hollow as a lung.

A man is fixing a carousel, a candy horse
is on its side. It seems to go
from curse to neck to man to coil.

And if god should enter this equation.

The stars at all hours.

Light too
through holes comes, through all the perforations.

Seven Lakes

Nothing brighter, the desert light

first thing. I want to be there

diving for pennies.

No one has died yet.

Every rosebush beside every fairway,

a mirage of your still life.

Quiet like a Cadillac

bronzing through the desert.

The unfinished paintings

passed down.

We sat in the backseat

and no one had to talk.

Elegance, succulence. The world

best left alone.

Draft Conclusions

Detraining or deplaning,
delaying
the inevitable.

Earth, you are a ghost maker.

I fear overheating
at the equator
and my longing for you.

The unsaid
trees unmeasured. The continent
has been mismapped.

What's done is done.

We will reforest
the forests

with medicine and moths
with see through wings.

The Weather Changed Around Us

The swell in our road, buckling,
was a season. Hauling trash.
I find the exhaustion
in any town.
But the maple air
around the maple tree,
breathe that.
Black equinox
upending a driveway.
Calves in a night dark barn.
March light through the cracks.
I don't miss the wind
off the lake. The loud geese
would be back by now, the loud crickets.

The Swallow Field

My well dressed homeless

relatives. Kitty corner from a gift shop.

Statuettes, the patron saints of architects,

protectors against

sudden death. Especially concerned with

weather and shelter, feeding the poor.

Across the street from

the sin washing fountain.

The poppies, bright matilijas,

as tall as I told you so.

A god you can only

listen for. His

last words to me were approving

of my outfit. Nice dress. Hand me down.

Convergence

My trust was worded
wrongly.
My words were energy spent.
Mass times the coefficient.
Proud figment.
Your eyes deep set.
There exists
a coordinate
whence we
first met.
Location
overlaid
with reason.
No calculation
to let go yet.
Lashes like ungulates.
Unarmed strength.
The planet has
no place for us.
No bed down nest.

Taxonomy

Patterned rain, little
fancy beetles,
will you
remember your name?
From first hatch
to fossil record,
shake me down.
A thousand insects
falling from one tree.
Minus extinction.
How long is once
around the sun?
Limb by limb
and busy to name
the species you inhabit.
Time succumbs
to its need for attention.
Dear Linnaeus,
the light is fiercest
between Cancer and Capricorn.
Is charismatic.

County Q

The tractor scrapes
muddy through the vetch.
With no proof no one believes

time is a hayfield.
It holds the center
around which we

are bent on fuss.
Echolalia, animal hoarding.
The imprecise
slumps of hay.

I am never perfection and this
is not the face I meant to make.

Summer's heavy
by the end. Birds, birds
whistling their bored song

like a bored waitress
bringing you your beer.
Bitter, porter, bitter, porter.
Are you ready? Are you ready?
Here we go. Here we go.

Ticket

The clearmind's attendant

discomfiture. Hard
bleachers. The magnified cold.

Even fear,
sit that down too.

We are surprised
with each willing

translation.
His willingness. That train

we are always on.

Index

The thymus decreases with age and thereby
the body's attempts to cope with fatigue. Shouldn't it be

greener by now? True
evolution requires a tweaking. One beak to turn the eggs
hourly.

One butterfly that looks
like one butterfly that tastes
strictly poisonous.

Everything that a flamingo does in its life, it does
flock minded. The first frequency of green ascending

the hillside leaf by leaf. One day I'll give up remembering.
You and I and the grass will grow.

Acknowledgements

To the editors of the following journals in which some of these poems first appeared: *Conduit, FIELD, Handsome, jubilat, The Volta,* as well as the anthology, *Buzz: Poets Respond to SWARM.*

To Kazim Ali, Stephen Motika, and Nightboat Books for their ethic and aesthetic.

To the estate of William Dole, my grandfather, for the use of the collage, *Second Architectural Fragment.* His work has been both map and compass.

To my teachers and elephant drivers. To my immediate kin. And to my alloy, Andrew and Haven. These are the love letters, as in please, as in thanks.

About Nightboat Books

Nightboat Books, a nonprofit organization, seeks to develop audiences for writers whose work resists convention and transcends boundaries. We publish books rich with poignancy, intelligence, and risk. Please visit our website, www.nightboat.org, to learn about our titles and how you can support our future publications.

This book was made possible by a grant from the Topanga Fund, which is dedicated to promoting the arts and literature of California.

The following individuals have supported the publication of this book. We thank them for their generosity and commitment to the mission of Nightboat Books:

Elizabeth Motika
Benjamin Taylor

In addition, this book has been made possible, in part, by grants from the National Endowment for the Arts and the New York State Council on the Arts Literature Program.

State of the Arts

NYSCA

ART WORKS.

National Endowment for the Arts
arts.gov